# Joyful, Grateful, Hopeful

A collection of poems by
Breyanna I.L. Evans

AzureStar Press
LLC

*Joyful, Grateful, Hopeful*

ISBN: 979-8-9907379-9-0 (Hardcover)
ISBN: 978-1-969618-00-0 (Paperback)
ISBN: 978-1-969618-01-7 (E-book)

Cover design and graphics © Breyanna I.L. Evans
Book design © Breyanna I.L. Evans
AzureStar Press, LLC

AzureStar Press
LLC

First print edition 2025.


breyannaevansauthor@gmail.com
breyannaevansauthor.com
@breyannailevans

*To Brandon and Oliver, who are very much the sunshine of my days.*

_Also by Breyanna I. L. Evans_

## YA Fantasy
Azure Light
Azure Light (Written under Breyanna I.L. James)
Crimson Darkness
Emerald Shadow

Bound Trilogy
Bound
Severed

## YA Fiction
Clairvoyance

## Children's Books
What I Do Know
Especially You

## Poetry
Accidentally External: A Poetry and Short Story Compilation
(Written under Breyanna I.L. James)

## Romance
Twice in a Lifetime

## Blog
"Writings" breyannaevansauthor.com

More books are always in the works for this author.
Join her newsletter to stay up to date with new releases by visiting
breyannaevansauthor.com.

# A Note From The Author:

Dear Reader,
　　The poems you read in this collection are not entirely representative of the kind of poetry I typically write. In other collections, you will likely find some poems like these, as well as a greater variety of poems that are darker or more mystical, and sometimes just nonsensical. However, I felt strongly that a work like this one, comprised of poems reflecting and highlighting things that make me feel joyful, grateful, and hopeful, was necessary in a time of the world that - to me - can feel entirely too dark. I hope you enjoy this change of pace for a while.
Keep reading. Keep living. Keep hoping.

Truly,
Breyanna I.L. Evans

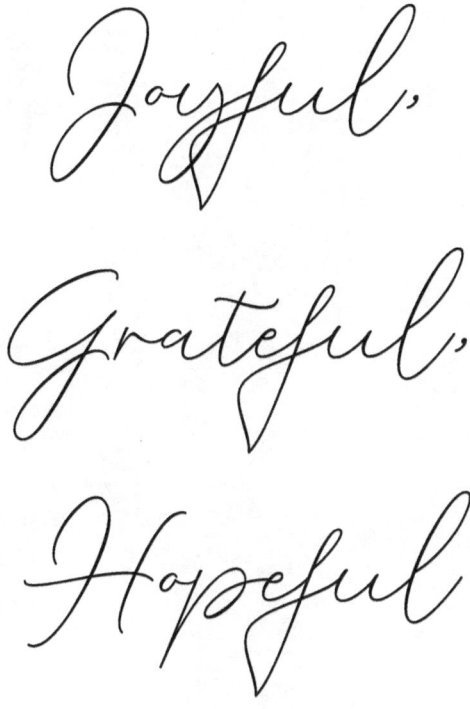

# Joyful, Grateful, Hopeful

A collection of poems by
Breyanna I.L. Evans

AzureStar Press LLC

Joyful

# THE SECOND START

The moment I knew was like only one other,
driving through the canyon in the dark...
I couldn't help the flutter in my stomach
or the way the beating picked up in my heart.

It felt the same as that night on the porch
all those many years and nights ago,
when I uttered those three words to you
that I'd never dared to say honestly before.

"I think I'm ready," I told you this time. Four words now, not three.
And we talked through the future on the way.
Though nothing yet had happened,
The decision was enough for us to say

someday,
we were going to have a baby.

## LIKE MOTHER

I love those
chalk dusted hands,
the uncapped markers,
and the tiny ink spills on the carpet...
The cheeks rosy from too much sun,
and a stick—I mean, a sword—in both hands.
I love the mud-caked shoes,
and curious squats as you analyze this flower,
and search for that bug.
I love the "Mommy, look!"
and the "Oh, gosh!"
You are just like your mommy.

## LIKE FATHER

I love that the moment you wake up, you call out to me,
not out of fear, but because you simply want to know that I'm here.
I adore your love of music.
I love that as soon as you're able,
you reach for the controller, turn on one console or another all by
yourself,
and ask, "Game?"
I love that you, smart baby,
can solve so many problems all on your own.
You astonish me.
You are, after all, your daddy's son.

# FINDING A MOMENT

I found a moment today
where I stepped outside and breathed the air,
touched the grass.
I took a moment today and
sat with my little one.
I could still
hear the distant sirens and horns,
but I could also hear
the whistling of the wind through the changing leaves,
and smell the dew-dampened earth,
and feel his chest rise and fall as he fell asleep
in my arms.
I recalled slow mornings
before he was big enough
and busy enough
to run around,
and I realized
just how rare these moments are.
I get them every day,
and I'm grateful for that,
but they are still in short bursts.
So, although I can hear the chaos of the outside world,
although I know he grows up a little more every day,
although there are still
emails to be answered
and projects to work on
and bills to pay
and things to plan,
I will take this moment
and work to find others just like it.

## BLOODBORNE TOGETHER

Intoxication of WinterLanterns,
their music
is a soft hum
taking the place if the roar
that usually appears
and my heart sings
as I traverse the nightmare with you.

# BRING YOUR KID TO WORK DAY

Something truly wonderful happened today.
I was working
and you came in
as you have been, lately
with your little self
and your big smile
and for half an hour,
you sat at my desk
and colored with me,
talked with me,
practiced your words as I worked on mine.
It was the best day at work
I've had
in a long time.

## PERFECT MORNINGS

I love to breathe in those first few moments of waking,
when lingering dreams dug at my consciousness.
My bedding is warm, soft, safe...
and you are at my side.
All is still, and our boy,
just one room over,
sleeps peacefully in his bed,
or plays quietly in his room
with his books.
Even better are the mornings
where there is no rush,
because it's the weekend.
There's no work to do,
no errands to run or bills to pay.
So we stay together,
basking in every perfect,
still moment.

## BUDDING LIFE

We talked of moving,
of planting roots in more fertile soil,
rich earth, where we can grow.
Where our boy can grow,
and our lives can begin.
I haven't been so excited in a long time.
The prospect buds in my chest
like a blossoming flower.

## MY BOY

My son, the sound of your laughter—
the sound of your imagination—
gives my heart wings.

I love to watch you play,
and explore,
and learn.
You are incredible.

## BUBBLES

All it takes is five minutes blowing bubbles with you in the sunshine,
with the birds chirping and fluttering overhead,
watching those iridescent, rainbow orbs rove through the air,
and seeing you chase after them, arms spread wide,
grinning uncontrollably, laughter bubbling up into the sky with
them...
to make me realize how wonderful you are,
and how important it is to take five minutes when you call
"Mommy!"
I realize that five minutes with you is everything to me.

# DREAMWALK

We walked along in dreams,
among the strobing lights
alongside fantastical creatures.
We stood beneath the shimmering, living,
thrumming flora
and watched our little one hover
over glowing crystals.
Transported to another realm.
This month's adventure was a Dreamwalk.

# FIRST TRY

Sometimes I look at the little human before me
and I see him grow.
I watch as he learns a new word or a new skill.
I watch a spark ignite within those big blue eyes,
and I'm truly amazed.
Awestricken,
because this incredible child here is the product of us.
Love.
Passion for learning,
and all the dorkiness a little body can contain.
I don't think we could have done any better.

# FEEDING THE DUCKS

Seeing you with the sunlight on your face,
that wide toothy grin revealing symmetrical dimples,
watching the rippling water as you call, "Ducky! Ducky!"
Waiting for your turn to feed them,
hearing that excited squeal as they gobble up their meal.
What an experience.
Thank you for reminding me how important it is to stop
and make time for the little moments
that add up to everything.

## HEARTACHE

Love.
It fills every fiber of my being.
It weaves our lives together.
Painful as it can be,
I am so grateful that I love you.

## THE JOURNEY

I walked along a lonely beach, my footprints in the sand
when a palm about my size fit itself inside my hand.
Now there were two walking along, our gazes to the sky...
next thing we knew were four paw prints that came rushing by.
Running along the coast were three and what there did I see,
but a set of tiny footprints that were racing alongside me.
I know one day the paw prints fade, the tiny toes morph to giant
shoes...
what once was one, then two, then four, will once again be two.

# FIREFLY HUNTING

I recall
traipsing around Stephen City
 at dusk, chasing fireflies,
and every time I caught sight
of their tiny flashing bodies,
you had looked away,
convinced
they weren't real.
But I saw their magic,
as real as that warm summer air,
as real as the freedom I felt
racing around the city,
admiring a new part of the world
with you at my side.

## SAY IT ALL

Tell me you love me, my dear, my dear,
as we wander the pathway together.
Tell me you will keep at bay my fear,
and that you will hold me forever.

Tell me you want me, my dear, my dear,
as you kiss me goodnight for a while.
Tell me it matters for you to hear
my laugh or to see me smile.

## INTERNAL

You have no idea
how deeply I cherish your smiles,
the games we play,
that silly laugh,
when too much air comes through your grin
in a broken hiss,
or when you reach out,
on the brink of sleep,
to pull my arms more tightly around you.

# A MOMENT

Sweet child,
with your doe eyes
and all the innocence in the world...
you make me so happy
when your laughter bubbles up,
weight free.

You have no outside worries yet,
so everything is wonderful.
Watching you drift off to sleep
with your tiny hand in mine
as you reach out each time I pull away,
because you just want me near you...
it's heaven.

I know you'll grow up,
and you won't always need me this way,
so I'll savor every moment we get together,
my baby.

# SLEDDING

Plastic shields of every color
whip down the slushy white blanket.
Sounds of laughter
and sometimes tears
jut out against the still, cold air
as fragile little puffs of white
flurry down from above,
and rosy cheeks,
and runny noses,
and chocolate cupcake smiles
make every second worth absorbing.

# BIRTH OF CHANGE

The world changed instantly and I was afraid
that all of my words would be poorly portrayed.
The world changed instantly when I gave birth
and all my priorities were shifted in worth.

# GARDEN SANCTUARY

Quiet joy
tranquility
standing in the Japanese gardens,
listening to the trickling water,
tiny drops of rain misting everything.
Everything green,
covered in moss,
still.
If you pause
for a moment,
you can breathe
the history
in the fresh air,
and you know you're a part
of something bigger. Out here,
we're all just visiting nature.

# I WALK

When I have a difficult decision,
or something's got me down,
when I need to work through hardships,
I wander through the town.

When I need to organize
the mess inside my head,
or I need to process,
I step outside and move as if pulled forward by a thread.

## PRECIOUS

Ah, to feel the sun on my face after days of cold,
icy winds, dark clouds and runny noses,
the sunlight is beautiful,
and so, so warm.

## CORTONA

I took a bite of wonder.
The sweet and savory spread across my tongue,
pulling at every emotion.

I tried something new,
crunch giving way to a soft center,
flaky and delicious.

Each dish brought me new emotions—
an experience, every one
transporting me to another country.

## BUILDING A PASSION

I love that I get to work every day
on the things I love.
I get to create stories.
Build characters.
Live their heartaches and victories
as they unfold on the page.
I love that I get to choose
what I want for my book,
and make my vision come to life.
I adore the process of finishing a story.
A design.
A work of heart...
then hold it in my hands
and share it with others who
will get the same thing out of
this thing I've created
that I got, and get,
out of the work of authors before me.
I carry a torch of my very own,
and the flame burns brighter
with each written word.

# WITH THE WATER

A soul
longing for connection
reaches out through water,
the world's bloodstream,
connecting every thing—
drawn to the clear liquid
that embraces skin and cloth,
earth and rock,
all the same.
Flow and motion...
a caress,
a support.
A whispering spirit—
dark in its own time—
but oh, the way it reflects and bends the light.

## COME SPRING

I stepped outside today
for a quick walk
after weeks of frigid weather,
and I felt like I could breathe again.
The warming air filled my lungs,
and although the breeze was still cool
and the grass and trees still hibernating,
I felt the possibilities
that the warmth would bring.

# PURITY

Small child bathed in sunlight.
Splashing in the rain.
Pure, Honest, Wonderful, Unfiltered.
No matter your scene,
there you are...
experiencing everything
as truly as possible.

## GOOD MORNING

Warm yellow light filters through the curtains,
landing on me.
Our child plays happily in the room beside ours.
There are a million thing to do today,
but nothing pressing.
In this moment, as I listen,
lying on a cloud of cotton sheets
with you breathing steadily at my side,
I stay.

## SLEEPY TIME

Some of my favorite moments of the day occur
around our sleepiest moments.
When I wake up to you calling my name softly from your bedroom,
not out of fear, but to let me know you're awake and ready to play.
 When I open your door, and I see you standing there,
teal blanket in one hand, your Fluffy in the other,
and the first thing you say is, "Hi, Mommy!"
Or after nap time, when I enter your room to wake you up
singing a silly song that always makes you look up at me
with that sleepy smile and a big stretch.
You always want to cuddle for the first few moments
as you fully wake.
Or at bedtime, our routine: Story, Zelda music, cuddles.
How I always have you repeat that you are safe and loved
and finish it off with something silly,
or how you always fall asleep with your hands on my face,
or in my hands.
Or afterward, the moments your dad and I share,
talking, bonding, curling up together.
In everything together.
My favorite times.

## STRANGE TODAY

It brings me great joy to get to know someone,
to learn their life story,
to know their struggles,
their passions...
but people don't open up that way these days,
and it seems strange to ask.

# DAYLIGHT

With the spring
and the melting ice
and the warmer winds
and the sprouting green
comes the reminder
that everything will be okay...
when I get off work
and I look outside;
and I can see the sun.

# GENUINE HUMAN CONNECTION

Oh, the joy of opening up,
connecting with another soul.
Sharing interests fills the cup.

## GROWTH

Almost nothing fills me
with more pure joy than getting better—
learning something new,
developing a skill.
It has always felt right,
and I know deep down to my core,
that I'm here to *learn.*

# I AM NOT A DESERT FLOWER

I didn't used to know better.
I knew no world but the one I was introduced to. Then...
...I flew
...I swam
...I drove
...I ran through the sand
...I stood in the ocean
...I breathed air that wasn't dry
...I danced in daily rain
...I wandered dense, green forests
...I saw color—bright greens, reds, oranges and blues
...I met new people who wanted to interact.
I am not a desert flower. I am a bird, and the world is my nest.

## DELIVERY

My heart nearly burst out of my chest when I saw
the truck pulling up in the drive.
Tan shorts and a package in arm broke the straw
bridge of composure, and I couldn't hide
the joy that I felt when I opened the box,
and glistening, gleaming inside
was the product of toiling like tilling rocks,
I stared at my book, beaming with pride.

Grateful

## THE WAYS YOU CARE

I am so grateful
to have you, my dear.
You never once grumble
about my restless legs
when we cuddle up at night.
Instead, you ask me about my pain,
and if I need a massage,
and you've always tolerated
that it takes me a year
to fall asleep every night.

## HOLDING FAST

I feel truly vulnerable
when I'm in your embrace,
and when our son is in mine.
The two of you have something magical,
and you are the only two people in this world
that I feel completely open with in those small moments.
That is something beautiful, pure,
and each time we hold each other close,
I feel it as deeply as if it were the first time.
I love you both.

## SLEEPING TOGETHER

It's simple, really.
I love sleeping with you.

I love climbing in bed with you,
pulling up the covers,
even when we're far too tired
to engage as lovers;
your presence is all the comfort I need.

I love waking up to find
that somewhere in the night
the two of us have wandered closer
to hold each other tight.
The pressure of your body against mine
 is wonderfully sweet.

I love that even unconsciously
we still find each other's hands.
Every day I wake up with you
at my side is sunny, bright, and grand.
Your groggy smile and morning cuddles...
Even when I'm laying down,
You sweep my off my feet.

# QUIET MOMENTS

They're not often found, at least not like this,
but I take them when I can.
Those moments when the world fades away...
When deadlines don't matter.

All that matters
is the breath I take and the air around me.

Alone, it's peaceful:
A time to reflect and ponder and *be*.
That's why I love walking so much.

With my baby boy, it's bittersweet
as I fight the wave of reminders that
I'm not here enough
and the worries that
I'm not doing enough,
that I've disappointed him somehow.

But here, in these moments,
as he curls up next to me and says,
"My mommy,"
all I feel is grateful.
Grateful to have such a wonderful kid.
Grateful to have a moment to hold him like this,
while I can.

With you, it's different still.
Our time together is thinner now
than it ever has been—
at least distraction free,

but I find myself so grateful every night
to be able to lay beside you,
close my eyes and feel
the warmth
of my favorite person beside me.

In these quiet moments,
I find myself feeling so truly blessed,
and I cling to every one.

# LOOKING BACK

I recall the days
that I couldn't see you.
The moments I counted down
until I got off work on Saturday afternoon
to drive seventy-five miles
to spend one night with you, one day
and return for another week,
or two,
or more,
counting down the moments until
I could make that drive again.
I recall how I felt,
how those embraces stopped the world from turning,
and how letting you go
and watching you watch me
as I pulled away from your home
to make the drive back
alone
always felt like
ripping a part of my heart away.
I still count down the moments, my dear,
until I get to see you again.
Only now, it's twenty paces
from the time I get off work
until the time I find myself in your arms,
and we can have lunch together,
spend our weekends together.
And now, I find myself grateful every night
to have the privilege of laying beside you,
of staying up talking face to face,
of falling asleep in your arms...

and every morning, rolling over
to see that you're still here.

We're still together,
no drive required.

# LONG WEEKENDS

When I was a kid,
I didn't appreciate the long weekends.
I loved school,
loved being in class,
and although I often enjoyed my summer breaks
(more time for reading, of course)
I barely noticed that those minutes and hours
were freedom,
beckoning me into a world
I hadn't experienced.

Now, I savor every hour of weekend I can get,
and every holiday,
every extended break.

I adore my work just as much
as I loved being in school,
but now, those moments away
are golden:
moments for me to be with my son,
to work on telling my own stories,
to be with my husband.

Those are wonderful, wonderful weekends.

# PICNIC

My sanctuary is on the mountaintop
...watching my boy
as he races carelessly through the grass.
"Be careful," I call to him, always,
but I well with pride at his childhood wonder.

...listening to the bubbling creek
as it flows past us,
and the sound of the wind
rustling the yellowing leaves.

The air is crisper here,
cleaner,
and every breath fills me with life I can feel.

The food is sweeter here,
as the three of us munch, letting the dog wander,
calling her back if she ventures too far.

In moments like these,
I'm grateful for the sunshine,
for nature,
for the moments I have to live with my family
*in the moment.*

# EFFECT OF YOU

Your kiss
is like a warm rain;
it covers my body like a blanket.
Your lips,
soft and gentle, but hungry...
Your touch
spreads wildfire across my skin.
To be held in your embrace
for an instant
is enough to stop
the world on its axis,
freeze time,
and make all the trouble melt away.

# CONNECTION

Talking with you is the greatest thing.
I love when we connect
and laugh
without distraction.
Even in times of stress,
you and I mesh so well together,
two sides of the same coin,
different, but connected.
I adore you.
I always have.
Your soul connected with mine,
your hand in my hand,
your arms around me,
fills me with the hope I need to move forward,
the love I need to feel whole,
the courage I need to dare.
My good wizard,
how you shape and cultivate my world,
the keystone
to my happiest, most magical days.

## NIGHT TERRORS

The screams in the night
aren't right,
and you are awake.
I rush to your side
and find
you're afraid.

You're nearly inconsolable,
as I lift you up
and hold you tight,
and we sit there rocking
through the night.

Borrowed pillows,
kinked neck, exhaustion that feels brand new,
and still, I'm so
grateful I could do this for you.

## LATE MORNING STROLL

There's nothing like
taking a late morning walk
under a crisp blue sky...
no wind, no worries.
The world is quiet
as you watch your rugrat
race around an empty ballpark
with the dog.

## MY LIGHT HOME

There they are, two beacons of light amid the void
two lighthouses beckoning me home
against a tumultuous black sea.

There they are,
two flashlights in the forest, my boys...
They light up my world wherever we are,
and lead me back home.

## HARD NIGHTS

I love the nights when one of us has a bad dream.
There's something truly beautiful about waking up for someone
and caring for them in your groggiest, most vulnerable, most
irritable state.
I love that we can be here for each other,
when our eyes won't open and our bodies drag with exhaustion,
beckoning us back to sleep.
Yet every time, we're there for each other,
comforting one another,
ensuring that everything is okay.
It was just a dream,
and we always fall back to sleep
together.

## YOU AND I

We are friends
sharing secrets,
naked truths.

We are soulmates,
connected to our roots.

We are lovers,
intertwining through and through.

We are partners.
I can do anything when I'm with you.

We are parents.
Together we try to raise him right.

We are guardians—
We hold each other through the night.

We are flames,
burning brightly in the dark.

We are candles,
ignited through the smallest spark.

We are intellects:
Through us ideas have a constant flow.

We are stars.
You, my darling, set my life aglow.

# THE RIGHT KIND OF STRONG

I am surrounded by women of all kinds:
Powerful women,
strong women,
caring women,
from all walks of life.
Mothers...
daughters...
friends.
Every one of them, resilient,
but not afraid to ask for help.
Kind, but firm.
Women who want it all – and *should*
want it all.

## A LITTLE GOES A LONG WAY

Look
how hard I'll always try.
The things I contribute.
Good talk, "Thanks, little guy,"
preoccupied now, shoo.

See
how easy it is to say,
"I appreciate you,
Good work; did well today...
...like the things you do."

## ODE TO HOME

You housed two kids just starting out,
allowed them to fill you with color,
a dog, and endless change.
You allowed them to change your yards,
tear town your walls.
You saw them through roommates,
pregnancy, childbirth,
early parenthood
and crazy toddlerhood.
And still you stood
reliable,
firm,
always here
for them to count on.

## MIDDAY NAP

I wasn't ready to wake up,
but I did,
because I had to.
My son was awake.

I didn't want to work today,
but I did,
because I care
about the work I do,
about the progress we make.

Despite the dragging lack of energy,
and the sore throat,
the muscle aches...
I moved forward,

and I was able
to take my lunch break
and get some rest.

I closed my eyes and,
finally,
I took a nap.

## "ADULTING"

The freedom of adulthood,
even with the responsibilities
of work
and raising children
and scheduling
and chasing dreams
and maintaining relationships,

I'm grateful.

I often hear that
adulting is hard,
and it is...

but it also brings some wonderful freedoms
like planning trips
and seeing the world,
and making your own choices
and purchases.

Being an adult can be challenging,
but I *still appreciate* all the freedom that comes with it.

## GRATITUDE

Life is too precious,
moments fleeting,
time ticking by in a blink.

So seize the moments, every single one.
You never know what could happen,
but you *will* miss what you waste.

# FROM AUTHOR TO READER

Thank you, wonderful readers.
You give my work purpose.
You take ink on paper,
or words on a screen,
and bring them to life.
You take endless hours of toiling and pondering
and make them meaningful.

# A BREATH OF FRESH AIR

I often find myself grateful for my lungs.
I'm an asthmatic.
I find I'm grateful for my heartbeat,
grateful to feel all the physical signals
that remind me—I'm alive.

## CONNECTED TO WORDS

The pen became the answer at a very early age.
I could see the stories leave me as I put them on the page.
The words became my savior through the hardships of my life:
They were my communication, my therapy, my scythe.

## RAIN

Not only does the rain
wash the earth
and fill the air
with the scent of a fresh start,
but it carries with it
every sentimental moment,
every rainy drive,
every walk in the warm summer drizzle,
every adventure,
every stormy reading day,
every tumble through the mud,
every moment I get with my baby boy.
Rain.
And like the puddles in the dipping, uneven sidewalks,
when it rains,
I am filled.

# VACATION DAYS

You and I have done something magical
with our time, my love.
Something that, growing up, I never imagined possible,
never knew it could be for me,
and now for my family.
We take vacation days.

We visit new places,
touch the sand on different coasts,
see the world from high above.
We count swimming poos in backyards as we pass them,
eat local foods and walk new paths.
We visit places with deep historical impact,
and talk with people who lead very different lives.

I recall us taking our boy to his very first beach...
How, at a year and four months old,
he had the same reaction
that I had at twenty three, the first time
I came in contact with the ocean.
We had to keep him out of the water,
but I couldn't blame him for struggling so hard to get back to it.
I'm the same way.

I love what we've done with our vacation days.
I hope we continue taking them for as long as we can.
Touch the sand in new places,
breathe the air in new spaces,
adventure and dance to new music,
while we can.

## GRAND MAN

For the man who brought us fishing,
who felt about as close to nature as anyone I'd yet seen,
for the man whose beard calmed and startled many,
for the big burly man who loved square dancing,
and kept at it.
For the man who,
even facing cancer and deep pain
and endless frustration at the cycle,
still wanted to talk,
share stories,
and crack ridiculous jokes.
We love you,
and we will miss you.
In the end,
I'm grateful that wherever you are,
you aren't suffering.
Thank you for teaching us,
over and over,
what strength looks like.

# WHO ARE WE, REALLY?

Life is about ebb and flow.
It's a million moments
all accumulated to create a grand picture.
Our actions, our words, the choices that we make...
It's who we are.
We are imperfect beings.
Flawed, impatient, selfish,
and yet,
we are inherently, unmistakably good.
What story will we tell
when our long day is through?
What greater image
will we leave behind?

## IT GOES SO FAST

Remember the time
when "remember the time"
was all that we could say?
Oh how we would reminisce days past,
we were living day to day.
Now we're so much more aware
of moments as they pass,
and thanks to our sweet little one,
they go now all too fast.
Now it's days instead of years
as we ask "remember when"
but we're much more conscious
of the time we spend.

## SLOW DOWN

If you focus on minutes
time will run out,
and you'll remember nothing at all,
but always feel rushed.

If you focus on *moments*
time won't matter.
Your memories will last,
and you'll remember to breathe it in.

Life is worth slowing down for.

This task, that appointment, those projects...
Ultimately,
none of it matters
when you pin it up against time.

# WHAT A JOB

Oh to be valued,
to be seen,
when colleagues around you
know your name,
your interests,
and care deeply.

They ask about your family,
and your personal endeavors,
and truly want to incorporate
the things you love to do
into your work.

Oh, to be seen,
to be valued,
when your boss
calls every once in a while
just to check on you
and tell you that
they see your efforts
and appreciate them.

# GRAND SCHEME

A man sat on the docks at the end of his life.
He pondered and daydreamed about his late wife.
He watched sunsets without her, wrote poems about her,
fed seagulls and watched the tides shifting without her.
He thought about time they spent laughing together,
how he thought they would share that same laughter forever.
He watched as the sun sank low in the sky
but couldn't bring himself to simply ask why,
why she had to go early, as he watched the clouds swirling,
and where she had gone as he hummed their love song.
Instead, he stood up with a nod of his head,
and he walked the shore home, and he climbed into bed.

Hopeful

## STRONGER TOGETHER

Darkness reaches in all around us, my love,
and here we sit
in a single spot of light,
clinging to each other out of hope instead of fright.
Head to chest and arms wrapped tight,
together, we will make it through this night.

People snatch away at us, at pieces of our hearts, my love,
and here we stand,
hand in gentle hand,
while leering sneering smiles lurk and soulless eyes will stare,
together, we will make it through this snare.

I will always hold you,
protect you from the dark,
scare away those who dare to say
that they would break your heart.
Together, my love, we stand against it all.
Together, we may change it.

# A SNOWY WALK

Today there was a sliver of sun,
just a moment of warmth in the cold.
I grabbed my family, and we went for some fun.
Before the wind returned, we were bold
with coats and hats and snow boots,
we trampled the brand new pathway
'til the cold wind returned
and so did we...
But I'll wait for another sunny day hopefully.

## RAISING A GOOD ONE

Every time my son hears me cough, or sneeze, he asks me,
"Are you okay?"
That's the kind of person I want to bring to the world—
the kind of person I want to be.
Every time he smiles, the world gets just a little bit brighter.

## WALKING TOGETHER

Warm sunlight speckles down upon us
as our feet drive us forward,
every step, progress.
We turn the corner and find
the lack of the near-constant icy breeze,
a moment of still air,
with the sun sprinkling down.
It reminds us,
if only for a moment,
that spring approaches.

## OUR LIFE

I refuse to waste my life
sitting and looking out the window
at a world that calls to me
without experiencing it.
I want to *live* the ocean with all my senses.
I long to hike the forests,
to watch my son grow
and live life alongside him...
learning,
playing,
growing.
I want to walk the streets and trails
with my partner's hand in mine,
knowing
that every sunset we watch,
every adventure we make time for
is *life* we've lived.

## BRIGHT AND COLORFUL

You are the moment
when the final bright rays of sunlight
shimmer down onto the land,
covering everything it touches in a rose gold hue...
so beautiful it seems rare,
but it's reliable.
I know the sun will set again this way,
just as I know I can count on you
to fill my world with vibrant color.

# THE THRUM

I fear the gray of everyday—
the mindlessness it offers.
I fear the fog and far away
that slithers in where lines blur.

I long for freedom and fresh air,
adventures, so I grasp them.
I wish for wild wind in my hair,
to let my curiosity stem,

and teach my son to chase the dream,
to not let blandness stop him,
and from the mountaintops we'll scream.
We seized days when we got them.

# THE SOCK

I *will not* be a sock to you,
there day after day
supporting you
comforting you
embracing you
and discarded when the day is through.

I *will not* be a sock to you,
never on your mind,
never what you want,
only chosen because I'm what you find...
put on, tucked away, and forgotten,
and discarded like I'm rotten.

It stinks.

## PERSPECTIVE

There comes a time when you look at things differently.
When plans change,
when it becomes important to reevaluate, and state
"These are not my principles.
My values.
My morals.
*This* is what's important to me."
But it is also vital
to stay true to those values...
Set boundaries.
Make time to acknowledge
and care for yourself.

SEASONAL

When the world blooms,
the doom in my heart
fades away for a while,
and I smile
and live and breathe.
Experiencing things
is easier,
less forced.
It gets worse in the cold.

But in the green,
life can be seen
and lived
and I can forgive
the longer, colder,
dreary days
that suck away
the joy and leave us barren
and searching

for sunnier days.

## DON'T WAIT

If you hear the call of the world,
don't wait.
If you want to go,
then go.
If you feel the pull,
follow that rope.
Life is short,
And you don't want to wake up one day
filled with regret
for all the things you never did.
Instead,
seize your moment.
Take the leap.
Run with that feeling.
Wake up one day
filled with memories
and joy
and love.

# THIS WOMAN IS PERFECT

She doesn't bleed,
and we don't see
the way she cries,
the way she fights
just to keep her life clean.

This woman is perfect.

She doesn't struggle,
doesn't fall
beneath the weight of it all.
It couldn't be
someone like she
has bad days just like me.

This woman is perfect.

Doesn't need help...
why would she scar
when things are never hard?
She never struggles to fall asleep
beneath the crushing chaos of it all.

She's a mother and a worker and a wife,
with the perfectly balanced life,
so we don't believe
don't listen when she says she needs...

a little time
a little love
a little help.

Why would we?

It's obvious to us
that she doesn't need it.

# SHIFTING TIDES

There comes a time when she doesn't want to try so hard anymore.
When she doesn't want to be the one to ask, to speak up.
There comes a time when she's tired of working so hard just to keep
things going.
When she grows tired of waiting.
When she says no more.
No more asking.
No more waiting.
No more talking.
No more praying to be seen,
to be the priority,
to be the motivation.
There comes a time when she's tired of being blamed,
tired of hearing she's "giving up when it's hard"
or that she "doesn't even try"
when it's *been* hard,
and she's *been* trying
and she's been the only one fighting for,
*clinging to*
the remnants,
the ghosts.
She deserves to be happy, too.
She deserves to be fought for.
She deserves to be put first once in a while.
To be asked,
to be waited for,
to be reached out to.
There comes a time for things to change
before they break.

## IS THAT TOO MUCH TO ASK?

I want a life full of love and positivity.
I want relationships that are about building each other up,
not tearing each other down or constantly comparing.
I want reciprocal trust and support.
I want unconditional love.
I want to build a life for my boy
filled with sunshine
and laughter
and deep, two sided conversations.
I want a family who shares mutual respect.
I want more.

# FRIENDLY FACES

I talked with people today...
strangers,
readers.
They passed by my table and we got to speak,
person to person
about all the wonderful parts of reading
and writing.
We just... talked.

That kind of human connection
seems rare these days, now that everything is online,
and I've been so stuck
seeing everyone's unhappy faces
that having this experience
brought some refreshing perspective.
Hope
that there are people out there
who do care,
and *want* to smile
and want to talk.

## MOTHER OF ALL

I stand in awe of the wilderness before me:
the towering trees,
the waves crashing against the rocks
and rolling jagged stone into sand,
the vast overgrowth.
For the first time in my life,
I feel hopeful that, though
we may not have as much wilderness as we once had—
and it's our fault—
but Mother Nature fights back
with a strength worth envying.
She is all around us, still,
and if we allow ourselves a moment of calm
to look around,
we can understand
her majesty.

# SEEK AND FIND

I put myself out there.
"We'll see," I said
and the excitement and fear
bounded round in my head.
I through out a hope
and what came bouncing back
was opportunity
written out big bold and black.

So I put myself out there
again, and I found
that more good things of all
shapes and sizes came round.
I sent out a line
and look what I caught—
another big chance,
fresh from the oven and still piping hot.

I'm starting to realize...
Yes, I'm starting to find
that the more that I learn and the more that I try
the more that comes back, and the more that I ask...
the more that I learn... I am up to the task.
The more on myself that I place a bet,
the more opportunities I seem to get.

## I'M HERE

When the wind howls
and darkness prowls
and you feel your body shaking...

When the streets curve
and you lose your nerve
and you feel your will is breaking...

Think of me.

When your stomach churns
and your world burns
and you don't know who to turn to...

When your thoughts rage
and your joints age
and your can't do what you yearn to...

Think of me.

When your heart breaks
and your soul aches
you've lost everything you once had...

When your words go
and you don't know
what will get you through all of this bad...

Think of me.

And

When the world's still
and you're peace-filled
and you're happy right where you are...

When your heart rings
and your mind sings
and you feel you're healing your scars...

Think of me.

## DREAM MADE TRUE

I dream
what could be
what can be
what will.
When dreams move me deeply
and stick with me still.

I dream
of what I want
what I can do,
and will.
When the dreams start to recur,
I feel a great thrill.

## SELF CARE

So many uncertainties...
Through my head they race.
What will happen if I find the most beautiful place?
What will happen if I let sunshine fall onto my face?
To them it may seem that this path I have won,
but they do not see all the hard work I've done.
What happens if I try to do what is right?
Will they stand in my path? Try to block out the light?
I don't wish to cut ties, and I know what I'll lose.
But I've got to remember: This is my life to choose.

## CHASE IT

If you know what you want, dear,
reach for it,
race toward it,
grasp it.

If you have a dream,
fight for it,
take it,
live it.

This is your life,
and it's your time.
You never know what will happen if you try,
but you could lose everything
if you don't.

# THINGS THAT REMIND ME

That crack in the sidewalk that yields to a tiny green stock.
That snail that made its way off the path without being crushed.
The mom who put herself through night classes
to pursue her dream.
The kid who goes to tutoring to learn how to read
after being in school all day.
That ray of sunshine that breaks through thick rainclouds.
That tree that grows between rocks on the cliffside.
These are all things that remind me
there is hope and strength all around.
Change may be scary. It can be difficult, certainly,
but it can also be so *good.*

## MORPHING AND MOVING ON

I am clay—
malleable.
I can change.

I am driven—
motivated.
I have the power to alter my circumstances.

Weather will shift;
moments will pass,
and no matter what,
life marches on.

So will I.

And I choose
to enjoy the view as I go.

## ALL NATURAL

Today, I watched a mother duck
keep six tiny ducklings out of harm's way.
She chased off other adults,
rounded up all six little kiddos,
and kept them together as they
hopped in and out of the water.
And I thought...
*That's a good mom, an attentive mom.*
It's wonderful to see that in the wild.
It reminds me that things can be naturally
and inherently good.

# TEMPORARY

The winter storm may freeze you,
the dark may settle in.
The icy winds may move you
when your strength is wearing thin.

But winter storms will settle,
and the sunlight will return...
and those frigid winds won't mettle
with a hot midsummer's burn.

## THE ROCK

Unmoving,
steady,
dependable.
Sturdy,
hard,
cold.
Seemingly impervious,
but slowly chipped away
with every subtle impact,
worn over time.

Rocks can be kicked and thrown away,
but together, they can build
a sturdy foundation
for something that reaches the sky.

## WILL

I thought that I couldn't,
and I was afraid,
so I didn't, I wouldn't,
and I wasn't brave.
I felt so unworthy, so I wouldn't try,
and my passion crept away to wither and die.

I thought that I could,
so I gave it a whirl...
didn't know what would happen—
I was just one girl.
But I toiled and I struggled,
and through it, I found
my work was unique
and worthwhile all around.

Well, it wasn't perfect...
It was lumpy, undone,
but it was my creation,
and through that, I won
the confidence that gave me
a chance I could take...
and I thought just maybe...
This life I could make.

# CRUMBLING HOME

When we were little, so full of wonder,
we didn't notice
the cracking tiles,
the peeling wallpaper,
the crumbling foundation...
the anger in the quiet,
the words left unsaid.
We didn't notice the plants that
were forcing their way through the splits in the driveway.
We didn't see
that the foundation we had
and would build our lives upon
wouldn't hold us up,
wouldn't stand against the weight of the
real world.
But we learned to observe,
to persevere
and keep going.
The home we had is long gone,
but *we* are still here.
We see it now, so let's learn
to patch the cracks,
to watch for decay,
to manage and guide the wild growth...
turn it into beautiful gardens.
We don't have to live
in a home that is crumbling.

# FLEETING

Breathe.
When the world seems to darken,
and the sun is nowhere to be seen.
Breathe.
When life feels it's caving in
and your walls are wearing thin.
Breathe.
When your doubt surrounds you,
and threatens to drown you.

In the grand scheme of things,
it's all simply passing moments,
so breathe.

## TURN THE PAGE

All things come to an end...

The good things, yes, it's true
but the fleeting nature of a passing moment
is the very thing that makes us pause to notice it.

The bad and difficult things fade, too,
but the darkness that we face
and the fear that pins us in place
is what makes that shining light in the distance so enticing.
We hold on to the hope that
someday,
this, too, will end.

We can turn the page,
and a new chapter will begin.

## ART

Life is comprised of little moments—
tiny glimmers of human beings
in brief interaction with one another.

Even solitarily,
every action, choice, and setting
defines the life that we live,

like a book is comprised of scenes and settings,
and a song, at its base, is comprised of notes,
just tiny measures of sounds.

# HUMAN BUT MORE

We are all human.
I forget that sometimes.
I forget that,
despite how much it looks like everyone else is fine,
that everyone else has it all together,
we all crumble.
We all have sorrow,
and guilt,
and doubts.
When we connect
as human beings
capable of seeing each others' fears,
we can be
anything.

## STILL MOVING

I am the water rushing by,
even when the world around me
is frozen.

## BESTIES

A wish,
a whisper,
a touch,
a look,
a sound,
a jitter,
a nervous tick,
a sigh,
a twitch,
a breath.
It amazes me how we know each other so well,
that we don't need words
to communicate.

## LIKE THE LAST

Every day is a chance...
an opportunity
to do better.

Every moment is a gift,
a chance to live.

Every choice is a blessing.
Can I make the right one?

Every laugh is a spark
that lights our way through the dark.

Every kiss is a reminder
to slow down
and pay attention...

because you never know
which will be your last,
so you might as well
make it count.

## MEANING

I am not the incidentals
or the inconsequentials.
I am the sum of my actions,
refractions
of the choices I make;
so let it be known
that I
—in all my glory—
am
at least in part
equivalent
to my multiple mistakes.

## ALL IT TAKES

The girl who couldn't
feared the pathway ahead
unknown
unshown,
so despite the pull,
she veiled it,
kept it hidden,
made her desire small...
and her dreams
happened only at night...
and then not at all.

It was all too easy
to let slip and fade to gray
the possibilities,
turned into *I-could-nevers*
and fear of failure
until forever
took them all away.

The girl who could
was also afraid
of the path she had not taken.
She couldn't see
anything more
than a dream,
a subtle pull made stronger
by the attention she paid to it
and the effort she made for it.

The girl who could

began to see small roads,
options, choices,
yesses and nos, that would shape her future
however she wanted them to.
Yes, there were failures,
and mistakes,
but lessons learned
that kept her going,
and made each victory that much sweeter.

They kept her dream from fading, or breaking,
ultimately taking
the shape of what she had so desired,
when it was all just a dream.

## ALL THE SAME

We are all people
soft,
driven my our emotions,
affected by our situations,
and when we peel back the layers...
uncertain.
Nobody has all the answers,
and it's okay that I don't.
Even if I fail,
I am not alone.
The amazing thing
is that,
like everyone else,
I have the ability
to try again.

# Acknowledgements

To Brandon, thank you for... well, everything. For your endless support. For inspiring me to write so many of these poems. For being someone I can share ideas with, brainstorm with. For someone who will give me honest critical feedback. For being my sunshine and my rainstorm. For reading my poetry, even when you don't get it.

To Oliver, for being my reason to reignite, to fight for my priorities, and for inspiring me every day to try and learn and grow.

To the incredible people I get to work with, thank you for encouragement and support, and for showing me the kind of person I can be.

To the bookstores that allow my books on the shelf, and to those who have requested my books! You have made my dream come true, and I am so grateful for all of you.

To the honest and positive writers within the Instagram community, thank you for lifting each other up. It's so important that we're here to encourage each other. To the amazing writers and reader's that I have met along the way, you are truly incredible, and even an act as simple as buying your next read or posting a review... well, it makes a world of difference to writers like me. Thank you for your passion.

To my writing group, thank you for helping me stay motivated. Our group chat is especially helpful in keeping the fire burning. Thank you for letting me geek out with you guys, and for doing this with me.

Lastly, to my fellow optimists. Keep that light burning. I see you, and I know how difficult it can be to be an optimist in a world full of pessimists and doubters. Just because you smile through the hard times and choose to look at things in a positive light doesn't mean that you're any less human. Remember that.

BREYANNA I.L. EVANS is a multi-genre author of several published books including children's stories, poetry, a novella, romance, fiction and fantasy, with more books always in the works.

After graduating with a bachelor's degree in creative writing from Utah Valley University, Breyanna taught middle school and high school English. She now works as a reading intervention specialist through the University of Utah Reading Clinic, always hoping to assist educators and struggling readers enhance their skills.

In her free time, Breyanna enjoys watching movies, painting, drawing, writing, reading, playing Dark Souls, and spending as much time as possible with her family. For release and book signing event updates, you can join Breyanna's email list at breyannaevansauthor.com

@breyannailevans
brevannaevansauthor@gmail.com
breyannaevansauthor.com

Enjoy the vibes in this collection?

Check out...

*Especially You:*
A rhyming children's book for everyone with the message that you can do anything... As long as you remain true to yourself.

*What I Do Know:*
A children's book for new parents and babies, reminding us that, no matter what we know... there is always more we can learn.

*Accidentally External:*
A dark and mysterious collection of poems, art and short stories by Breyanna I.L. Evans (James)

What's coming next?

The Boy and the Stone
Coming December 2025